Building Wealth in the Crypto Economy

How to Build a 6–7 Figure Portfolio Using Strategy, Patience, and Asymmetric Investing

By Joe Correa

Published by Live Stronger Faster

This book is for educational and informational purposes only. The author and publisher are not engaged in rendering legal, financial, or other professional advice. Readers should consult a qualified professional before making any financial decisions.

First Edition

Table of Contents

Introduction

There are moments in history when a new form of wealth is created — and most people miss it. Not because the opportunity wasn't real or available, but because they didn't recognize the signals, didn't prepare, or were too paralyzed by fear and doubt to act. We are living through one of those moments right now. The cryptocurrency economy, often dismissed as volatile or speculative, has evolved into a new frontier of asymmetric wealth creation — where the rules are being rewritten and the gatekeepers of the old financial world are losing power. This is not just a technological revolution. It's an economic revolution. And it's your opportunity to play offense instead of defense.

In the traditional world, wealth has been built slowly — through long careers, real estate holdings, or equity in businesses passed down through generations. These remain valid paths, but crypto introduced a new paradigm: one where everyday people — with no connections, no inherited wealth, and no Wall Street experience — have been able to build six, even seven-figure portfolios starting with just a few hundred dollars and a willingness to learn. The stories of 10x, 100x, and even 1000x gains aren't myths — they're mathematical realities in a space built on exponential growth. But building wealth here is not about luck or hype. It's about knowing how to make small, strategic bets with massive upside potential. It's about understanding cycles, managing risk, and thinking decades ahead in an economy that moves at the speed of code.

This book is about taking control of your financial destiny using the most powerful financial tool of our time: asymmetric investing in the crypto economy. But let's be clear — this is not a "get rich quick" guide. In fact, if that's what you're looking for, you're in the wrong place. This is a blueprint for thoughtful, strategic wealth building. It's about compounding your wins, protecting your capital, and positioning yourself to thrive across cycles. Whether you're entering the market for the first time or refining a portfolio you've already built, the goal here is to help you think, act, and grow like a digital-age wealth builder.

What separates the winners in crypto from the masses isn't just technical knowledge — it's mindset. The investor who understands asymmetric opportunity can stomach short-term pain for long-term gain. They understand that most of the world is playing defense: reacting to market fear, selling too soon, chasing trends. True wealth builders play offense — they move strategically, rebalance when others panic, and set long-range targets most won't even consider. They know that success doesn't come from catching the top or bottom of the market, but from sticking to a plan when it feels most uncomfortable to do so. They don't let red candles shake them. They let data guide them. And when the next major wave comes, they're already positioned.

Throughout this book, you'll learn how to structure your portfolio in a way that reflects your risk tolerance, goals, and timeframe. You'll see how to use crypto's volatility to your advantage, not your ruin. You'll discover real-world case studies of individuals who turned modest investments into life-changing wealth — not through blind luck, but through consistency and courage. We'll also discuss the psychological traps that destroy most portfolios — greed, fear, impatience — and how to guard yourself against them. And perhaps most importantly, you'll learn how to translate your crypto gains into tangible, real-world value — whether it's reinvested income, financial freedom, or a legacy that outlives you.

The wealth-building process in crypto has phases: accumulation, growth, preservation, and eventual deployment or exit. Each phase requires different strategies, tools, and disciplines. In the early stages, you're focused on identifying undervalued assets and consistently investing small amounts. In the growth stage, you might leverage market cycles, staking rewards, or yield-bearing assets. As your portfolio matures, your focus shifts to protection — diversification, risk reduction, and hedging. And finally, you must decide how and when to take profits, convert to real assets, or compound into new opportunities. This book will walk you through each of these stages in detail, giving you a holistic, long-term playbook for financial sovereignty.

We're not just talking about buying tokens. We're talking about buying freedom. The freedom to walk away from jobs that no longer serve you. The freedom to live where you want, work how you want, and give how you want. The freedom to build a life that aligns with your values, not just your paycheck. That's what true wealth is — not just numbers on a screen, but options, autonomy, and peace of mind. Crypto is not a lottery ticket. It's a tool. And like any tool, it can build a masterpiece or cause destruction — depending on how it's used.

So, whether you're sitting on a few coins and wondering what to do next, or whether you're ready to build a seven-figure plan that stands the test of time, this book is your roadmap. You don't need to time the market perfectly. You don't need to be a programmer or a trader. You just need the right mindset, strategy, and consistency. You need to treat crypto wealth like a long game — because that's how the legends are made.

Let's begin your next chapter. Not just in this book — but in your wealth story. You have access to one of the greatest financial opportunities in history. What you do next will define your future.

Let's build wealth — the smart, strategic, and sovereign way.

Chapter 1: The Wealth-Building Mindset in Crypto

Wealth is not just about money — it's about how you think. And in the crypto world, mindset is everything. The rapid pace, constant volatility, and emotional rollercoaster of the digital asset market tend to shake out those who treat it like a casino or chase the next quick win. But those who approach it with a wealth-builder's mindset — grounded, strategic, and forward-looking — are the ones who consistently grow their portfolio year after year. Before we dive into allocations, tools, or asymmetric strategies, we must begin with the one thing that determines your long-term success: how you think.

The wealth-building mindset begins with **patience**. Crypto is a space of extremes — wild gains and devastating losses — often within the same week. This volatility makes headlines, but real wealth is built in the in-between moments: the quiet accumulation during bear markets, the disciplined holding during uptrends, and the unemotional profit-taking at peaks. Patience allows you to see beyond the moment and focus on the long-term horizon. It's what separates those who panic sell from those who buy when everyone else is afraid. Those who succeed in crypto view time as their greatest advantage — not timing.

Another key trait of the wealth-building mindset is **conviction through education**. The average investor makes decisions based on price action or hype. But the wealth builder makes decisions based on understanding. They study the whitepapers. They follow macro trends. They learn the tokenomics. They understand not just *what* they're buying, but *why* it has long-term value. This depth of knowledge creates resilience. When the market dips 40% in a month, the educated investor doesn't panic — they rebalance. Because they know what they own, and they believe in the underlying technology or protocol. Wealth in crypto isn't just about picking winners — it's about having the confidence to hold them through storms.

Then comes **emotional discipline**, a rare trait in crypto. It's easy to feel euphoric when your portfolio doubles in a week. It's just as easy to feel devastated when it loses half its value. Both emotions — greed and fear — are the enemy of strategy. A wealth builder trains themselves to detach from short-term emotions and stick to the plan. They set price targets ahead of time and follow them. They don't chase pumps. They don't FOMO into the latest meme coin. They understand that most of the damage to portfolios isn't caused by bear markets — it's caused by undisciplined decisions made in response to them. Building wealth means managing yourself, not just your assets.

The most powerful trait of the crypto wealth mindset is **asymmetric thinking** – the ability to see that you don't need to risk everything to win big. You just need to place small, strategic bets on the right ideas. In traditional finance, you might invest for a 10% annual return. In crypto, it's possible to get 10x over several years – not through gambling, but through early positioning. This means being willing to allocate a small portion of your capital toward high-risk, high-reward opportunities – projects with strong fundamentals, emerging narratives, or long-term utility. It also means being willing to lose small to win big. Asymmetric investors understand that one or two correct moves can change their life, even if they have several small losses along the way.

A true wealth-builder in the crypto space also understands the concept of **cycles**. Nothing in this market goes up forever, and nothing stays down forever either. Bitcoin moves in four-year halving cycles, altcoins follow with amplified volatility, and major narratives rotate based on macro shifts, regulation, and adoption. Instead of reacting emotionally, the strategic investor *prepares* for each phase. They accumulate when others are selling, consolidate gains when euphoria peaks, and build dry powder for the next wave. They recognize the signs of the market – and they act like professionals, not tourists.

You'll also need to develop **long-term vision**. Ask yourself: *Where is this space going in 5, 10, or 15 years?* The smart money isn't just thinking about today's gains — they're positioning for the next internet. For the digitization of finance. For global access to decentralized systems. The wealth-builder is thinking about tokenized real estate, decentralized AI, DAOs, and the eventual onboarding of billions of people into crypto — many of whom don't even know what a wallet is yet. That kind of vision lets you endure short-term volatility because you understand the seismic shift that's still unfolding.

And lastly, you must have **a strategy, not just hope**. Wealth building isn't just holding — it's rebalancing, taking profits, diversifying, and protecting capital. It means having exit plans. It means understanding tax impact. It means asking, *"What will I do with my gains once I have them?"* A portfolio without a plan is just a gamble with good intentions. But a plan — even a simple one — gives you structure, reduces stress, and increases your chances of long-term success.

In the chapters that follow, we'll break down how to build, manage, and grow a six-to-seven-figure crypto portfolio. We'll look at allocations, tools, market behavior, and wealth strategies adapted to the digital age. But none of it matters if you don't build your foundation first — your mindset. The greatest gains in crypto are often psychological. Master your emotions, upgrade your thinking, and treat your wealth journey like a business — not a game.

Remember: in crypto, you don't need to be the smartest person in the room. You just need to be the calmest. The most prepared. The most consistent. Because while others are chasing, you'll be building. Quietly. Strategically. Powerfully. And that's how real wealth is made — not overnight, but over time, with intention.

Javier's freedom story

Javier was no stranger to hard work. A 38-year-old father of two, he had spent the past 15 years working in IT, living paycheck to paycheck, saving modestly into a retirement account that always seemed to lag behind inflation. In 2020, while stuck at home during the global lockdown, Javier stumbled across a Reddit post talking about Bitcoin. At first, he dismissed it — he had heard about it years earlier and figured he'd already missed the boat. But something about the way people were speaking about decentralization, limited supply, and independence from traditional banking caught his attention. He didn't jump in right away, but that thread sparked a curiosity that slowly began to change his life.

For the next several weeks, Javier found himself deep in YouTube videos, blog articles, whitepapers, and podcasts. Not the hyped-up influencer stuff, but deep dives into the technology, the monetary philosophy, and the vision behind this new digital economy. The more he learned, the more he realized crypto wasn't just about money — it was about freedom. It was about leveling the playing field. And for someone who had always felt like he was playing catch-up in a rigged system, that message hit home.

But Javier didn't make his first investment out of excitement. He made it from strategy. He had seen too many people jump into tech stocks or real estate fads too late, without a plan. So he sat down one evening with a spreadsheet, a notebook, and a simple goal: to build long-term wealth in a space that was still in its infancy. He decided he would treat crypto like a business — not a gamble. He would start with small, regular investments and only put in what he could afford to lose. Most importantly, he made a promise to himself that he wouldn't be swayed by panic or hype.

His first buy was a modest $250 in Bitcoin. A week later, he bought $250 of Ethereum. Then, he began researching altcoins with real utility — coins that solved actual problems or were building real infrastructure. He didn't chase meme coins or TikTok hype. He chased fundamentals. He set alerts. He learned to read charts just enough to identify support and resistance. He studied market cycles. He ignored the noise.

Three months later, the market dipped. Hard. Javier's $2,000 investment was suddenly worth $1,200. He felt the sting of fear rising – that tight feeling in the chest, the urge to "cut losses" and run. But instead of acting on emotion, he returned to his notes. He re-read the whitepapers. He listened to interviews with developers. He reminded himself why he invested in the first place. Then, instead of selling, he bought more.

This became his rhythm. Buy. Study. Reflect. Rebalance. He never overextended himself. He never stopped learning. And he started to notice something unusual – while many of his friends were stressing about inflation, layoffs, and the stock market, Javier was calm. Empowered. Not because he had made a fortune – yet – but because he had a plan and believed in what he was building. He was thinking five years ahead while others were thinking about next Friday.

Two years later, his strategy began to bear fruit. His $15,000 total investment had grown to over $120,000. Some coins had gone 3x, others 10x. A few had flopped – but he had never bet too heavily on any single project. His consistent, diversified, long-term mindset had insulated him from destruction and positioned him for growth. During the next bull run, his portfolio crossed $300,000. He could hardly believe it. But instead of celebrating wildly, he rebalanced. He took profits. He moved some into stablecoins. He paid down debt. He didn't YOLO into the next big thing — he stayed the course.

Javier's story isn't about luck. It's about mindset. It's about the quiet power of patience in a world obsessed with instant gratification. It's about the courage to invest when others are fearful, and the humility to learn when others are shouting. Most importantly, it's about seeing wealth not as a destination — but as a behavior.

Today, Javier continues to build his portfolio. He still works, but with more freedom — using remote contracts, traveling with his family, and spending less time worrying about money. He's also helping others — teaching his sister how to buy her first wallet, guiding his coworkers on the basics of dollar-cost averaging, and hosting a small meetup at his local library on "How to Build Wealth with Crypto Safely." He's not a millionaire — yet. But he's wealthier in the ways that count. He's in control of his financial future. He's building something that can last.

Javier's mindset — patient, strategic, curious, and committed — is exactly what separates long-term winners in the crypto economy from everyone else. It's not the token you choose. It's the habits you build. And in a world that changes faster than ever before, mindset is the one investment you can never afford to ignore.

Chapter 2: The Asymmetric Opportunity of Crypto

One of the most powerful concepts in the world of investing is *asymmetry*. In simple terms, asymmetric investing means risking a small amount of capital for the potential of an outsized return. It's the opposite of what most people do – risking everything to gain a little. And nowhere is this principle more alive and accessible than in the crypto economy. While traditional markets often reward the well-connected and capital-rich, crypto has created a space where anyone, anywhere, with as little as a hundred dollars and the right knowledge, can make life-changing gains. The opportunity is asymmetric – and it favors the prepared.

Asymmetric investing is not gambling. It's not buying every low-cap altcoin hoping for a moonshot. It's a strategic, disciplined approach to finding projects, trends, or assets where the **potential upside dramatically outweighs the downside**. In crypto, this might mean putting 1% to 5% of your portfolio into a project that could 10x or even 100x if successful, while being comfortable with the idea that it may also go to zero. The goal isn't to win every time – the goal is to position yourself so that even one win can more than offset several losses. This is how angel investors build fortunes in startups. It's also how smart crypto investors build generational wealth.

Let's break this down further. Suppose you allocate $500 across 10 different early-stage projects, putting $50 into each. If just one of them returns 20x and the others all fail, you've turned your $500 into $1,000. If two succeed, you've doubled or tripled your capital. If five break even and one moons, you're still ahead. That's the beauty of asymmetry — the risk is capped, but the reward is exponential. Compare that to traditional investing where people often risk $100,000 to earn 5% annually — a gain of just $5,000 per year. Crypto flips that equation.

The key, however, is **selective exposure**. You don't put your entire portfolio into asymmetric bets. Instead, you carve out a small but significant percentage — usually between 5% and 20%, depending on your risk tolerance — and treat it like a high-risk, high-reward innovation fund. The rest of your portfolio can be in larger-cap assets like Bitcoin, Ethereum, or stablecoins earning yield. This allows you to play the upside while protecting your core capital. Asymmetric investing is not about going all in — it's about stacking the odds in your favor, intelligently and repeatedly.

What makes crypto so uniquely suited for asymmetric opportunity is the **early-stage nature** of most projects. In traditional markets, by the time the average investor hears about a company, the biggest gains are already gone. IPOs are often priced for institutional insiders. In crypto, however, many projects launch directly to the public via decentralized exchanges or token launches. This means that with the right timing and research, you can be early — sometimes earlier than venture capitalists. This is a rare and powerful position that doesn't exist in most other asset classes.

But to capitalize on this opportunity, you must also understand **asymmetric information**. In traditional finance, valuable information is guarded. In crypto, it's often hiding in plain sight. Discord groups, GitHub commits, community activity, developer updates, and on-chain metrics can tell you a great deal about a project's health and momentum — if you know where to look. Most people ignore these signals because they take effort to understand. But effort is a form of leverage. The more you learn, the more you can see value before the crowd does. And in a space where speed matters, being early can be the difference between a 2x gain and a 50x life-changer.

It's also important to recognize that asymmetric investing requires **emotional tolerance**. You will see wild price swings. You will experience drawdowns. You will doubt your positions. This is part of the game. If you treat every investment like your entire financial future depends on it, you'll panic at every red candle. But if you allocate with intention, accepting that some bets will fail, you'll have the clarity to hold the winners and cut the losers without emotional attachment. That clarity is your edge.

Timing plays a critical role in asymmetric gains. The **early stages of adoption**, just before a trend goes mainstream, are often the most profitable windows. This is where you find tokens that are undervalued relative to their future utility. Consider the rise of DeFi, NFTs, Layer 2 scaling solutions, or Real World Asset (RWA) tokenization. The investors who got in early during the research and experimentation phases made asymmetric returns. Those who waited until mass media picked up the story usually entered at or near the top. Asymmetric investing rewards foresight — not hindsight.

To succeed in this game, develop your **asymmetric thesis**. This is a set of ideas or narratives you believe in deeply, supported by research, where you're willing to allocate small, calculated positions. Maybe it's the growth of decentralized AI. Maybe it's privacy coins in a surveillance-heavy world. Maybe it's tokenized carbon credits, cross-border remittances, or decentralized identity. Pick the themes you understand best and focus on them. Learn the leaders. Join the communities. Stay engaged. When the market comes around to your thesis — and it will — you'll already be positioned.

Finally, think of asymmetric investing as a **long-term strategy**, not a series of quick flips. The biggest gains often take years, not weeks. Consider early Bitcoin or Ethereum adopters. They saw their portfolios swing violently, but those who held through cycles and continued to accumulate ended up with life-changing wealth. The secret wasn't just in picking the right asset — it was in *holding through the storm.* Asymmetry is not just about numbers — it's about mindset, patience, and conviction.

In the next chapter, we'll break down how to apply this mindset to your actual portfolio — building a 6- or 7-figure crypto wealth strategy with specific allocations, tools, and examples. But always remember: in the asymmetric game, you don't need to be right often — just big when you are.

How Fatima went from freelancer to investor

Fatima was a 29-year-old freelance designer living in Morocco. She had always dreamed of financial independence but grew up in a household where investing felt like something only the wealthy or Western-educated could do. Banks were untrustworthy, inflation eroded savings, and opportunities were scarce. Yet, Fatima was curious. She followed tech trends, dabbled in online business, and occasionally stumbled across conversations on Twitter about people making extraordinary gains with crypto. Still, she hesitated — until one day, she came across a podcast that introduced her to the concept of asymmetric investing.

The idea struck her like lightning. It wasn't about risking everything for fast money. It was about betting small and smart — risking what she could afford to lose for the chance of gaining much more. Fatima realized she didn't need to start with thousands of dollars or a degree in finance. She just needed a plan and the courage to start small. That night, she opened her first exchange account. With the equivalent of $300 in local currency, she bought a mix of Bitcoin and Ethereum, then reserved a portion — $50 — to explore emerging projects she believed in.

Fatima dove deep into research. She explored Discord communities, read whitepapers on tokenized freelance platforms, and joined a DAO focused on global gig workers. One project — a decentralized design marketplace — captured her attention. It wasn't popular yet. No YouTube influencers were talking about it. But she resonated with the vision: giving designers in emerging countries direct access to clients through blockchain-based payments. She bought a small amount of the token, not because it was trending, but because she *understood* it. That became her asymmetric bet.

Months passed, and the market turned sour. Bitcoin dropped 30%. Most altcoins were down even more. Her portfolio shrank. But Fatima didn't panic. She understood volatility was part of the journey. She rebalanced and used the dip to add slightly more to her highest conviction projects. As she worked on freelance gigs, she kept learning — watching market cycles, exploring tokenomics, and following real adoption. While others were obsessed with price charts, she was focused on building knowledge and finding undervalued ideas hiding in plain sight.

Then it happened. The design token she believed in started gaining traction. Influencers caught on. Exchanges listed it. Usage exploded. In a few months, the token 25x'd. Her modest $50 was now worth over $1,200. It wasn't a fortune, but it was proof. Asymmetric investing worked. One small, well-researched move had outperformed her entire savings account. And even more important — it had changed her mindset forever.

Fatima didn't stop there. She began treating her portfolio like a multi-tier system. Her core was stable — BTC, ETH, and a few blue-chip assets. Then she had her asymmetric layer — 5% to

10% of her capital set aside for bold, high-upside bets. Some flopped. A few stagnated. But one or two others – including a DeFi project from Latin America and a zero-knowledge privacy coin – returned massive gains. Not because she was lucky, but because she studied the technology, the teams, and the user growth long before it went mainstream.

Today, Fatima earns in crypto, saves in crypto, and invests in crypto. Her modest asymmetric plays gave her enough capital to take a break from work, build a website design agency, and start teaching other young people in North Africa how to approach crypto strategically. She doesn't brag about moonshots or pump coins. She teaches the power of small, educated risks. The magic of asymmetric investing isn't just in the gains – it's in how it transforms your worldview. Suddenly, you no longer feel powerless in the financial system. You feel like a participant. A player. A builder.

Fatima's story reminds us that the best investments aren't always the loudest ones. They're often the projects that quietly solve real problems, led by dedicated teams and overlooked by the masses. When approached with humility, discipline, and vision, asymmetric investing in crypto isn't just a wealth strategy – it's a doorway to freedom. For those willing to do the work, think independently, and act decisively, the upside is more than just financial. It's personal. It's transformational. And it's waiting.

Chapter 3: The 6-Figure Crypto Portfolio Blueprint

Building a six-figure crypto portfolio is not the result of one lucky trade – it's the result of a structured, intentional strategy applied over time. The majority of people in the crypto space chase profits but rarely build wealth because they lack a plan. In this chapter, we're going to break down exactly how to structure a portfolio that can grow to $100,000 and beyond. Whether you're starting with $1,000 or $25,000, the principles remain the same: protect your capital, invest with intention, and let compounding do the heavy lifting.

At the core of this blueprint is the idea of **allocation** – how you divide your money across various crypto assets. Every great portfolio starts with a foundation. For most investors, that foundation is **Bitcoin (BTC)** and **Ethereum (ETH)** – the two most established, liquid, and secure digital assets in the space. These should typically make up 40% to 60% of your portfolio, depending on your risk tolerance. Bitcoin acts as a store of value and hedge against inflation, while Ethereum offers exposure to the broader ecosystem of smart contracts, DeFi, and NFTs.

Once your foundation is in place, the next layer consists of **mid-cap altcoins** with strong fundamentals, real utility, and active development. These might include Layer 1 and Layer 2 solutions like Solana, Avalanche, or Arbitrum; DeFi protocols like Aave or Curve; or infrastructure tokens like Chainlink or The Graph. This portion of your portfolio — usually 20% to 30% — is where you capture higher growth while still maintaining a reasonable risk profile. These assets may experience greater volatility, but they also have significantly more upside than BTC or ETH during bull cycles.

Then comes your **asymmetric layer** — the high-risk, high-reward portion of your portfolio that includes early-stage projects, low-cap tokens, and trend plays. This should be no more than 10% to 20% of your total portfolio and should be diversified across several bets. This is where the biggest returns are possible — 10x, 50x, or even more — but also where losses are common. By keeping your allocation limited, you reduce the chance of catastrophic loss while keeping the door open to explosive growth. Every six-figure portfolio you've heard about likely had one or two successful asymmetric plays that did the heavy lifting.

A well-structured portfolio also includes a **cash or stablecoin reserve** — typically 5% to 15%. This is your dry powder for market crashes, dips, or sudden opportunities. Holding stablecoins like USDC or USDT on the sidelines may seem unproductive during a bull market, but during corrections, they become your most powerful tool. The ability to buy when others are fearful — and to do so without selling your winners — is one of the strongest advantages a disciplined investor can have. Cash is not just capital. It's confidence.

Next is the concept of **dollar-cost averaging (DCA)**. Rather than trying to time the market, DCA means investing a fixed amount of money at regular intervals — regardless of price. This strategy smooths out your entry points, reduces emotional decision-making, and builds consistency. Whether it's $50 per week or $500 per month, automating your contributions removes the guesswork and builds your portfolio steadily. Over time, you'll accumulate more during downtrends and less during peaks — a natural way to "buy low."

Rebalancing is another essential practice in growing your portfolio. As markets move, your allocations will shift. For example, if one asset grows faster than others, it may balloon to take up 50% of your portfolio. Rebalancing means periodically selling a portion of that asset and redistributing it to bring your portfolio back in line with your original strategy. This practice locks in gains and prevents overexposure to a single asset. A good cadence is to rebalance every 3 to 6 months, or when a position exceeds your pre-set limits.

One often-overlooked factor in portfolio growth is **compounding**. When you earn yield through staking, lending, or liquidity providing — and reinvest those rewards — you accelerate your portfolio's growth. Even small percentages compounded monthly can result in massive gains over a few years. DeFi platforms offer ways to earn 4%–20% APY (and sometimes more) by simply putting your crypto to work. However, always assess the **smart contract risk** and stick with trusted protocols.

Now let's talk numbers. Suppose you start with $5,000 and add $500 monthly while achieving a modest 20% average annual return — conservative by crypto standards. In five years, you'd have over $60,000. If you get lucky with a couple of 10x asymmetric plays during a bull cycle and take profits intelligently, your portfolio could easily cross $100,000. The key is consistency — sticking to your strategy and avoiding emotional decisions that sabotage long-term gains.

Lastly, don't forget your **exit strategy**. Many people build great portfolios and lose it all because they don't know when or how to take profits. Set milestones ahead of time. For example, "I will sell 25% of this position if it 3x's," or "I'll move profits into stablecoins after I reach $100,000." Protect your gains. Real wealth is built when profits are captured and either reinvested or used to improve your life. Don't let greed erase years of smart investing.

This six-figure blueprint is simple, but not easy. It requires discipline, emotional control, and a long-term vision. But if you follow it – adjusting based on your own goals, timeline, and risk appetite – you'll be far ahead of 90% of crypto investors. Remember: building wealth isn't about hitting home runs. It's about stacking base hits, avoiding big mistakes, and letting time do its job.

How Marcus' life changed with crypto

Marcus lived in Chicago and worked as a logistics manager for a local trucking company. He was practical, responsible, and never considered himself a "finance guy." He didn't grow up around money and had always followed the conventional wisdom: save 10%, invest in mutual funds, retire at 65. But by his late 30s, that plan wasn't working. His savings grew slowly, inflation kept chipping away, and despite years of hard work, financial freedom felt out of reach.

In 2021, a co-worker introduced Marcus to crypto during a lunch break. At first, Marcus brushed it off as a fad – he'd heard about people losing everything. But his curiosity got the better of him. That night, he read about Bitcoin, Ethereum, and how decentralized finance was allowing people to grow their capital outside traditional systems. He wasn't ready to jump in, but the seed was planted. Over the next few weeks, Marcus researched portfolios, listened to podcasts, and discovered a strategy that spoke to him: a structured, layered crypto portfolio built for long-term growth.

He started small. With a $10,000 savings cushion, Marcus committed to investing just $3,000 in crypto — enough to feel it, but not enough to hurt if it went south. He built a spreadsheet, divided his budget, and created a simple but strategic plan. He allocated 50% to the foundation — Bitcoin and Ethereum — assets he understood and trusted. They didn't promise overnight riches, but they had history, utility, and institutional adoption.

Then came the next layer — promising altcoins with real utility. He chose a few based on use cases that made sense to him: decentralized storage, gaming ecosystems, cross-chain bridges. He spent evenings reading whitepapers and watching developer interviews instead of Netflix. He didn't chase whatever was trending that day. He built conviction through understanding.

For the final 15% of his portfolio, Marcus allowed himself to be bold. These were his asymmetric bets — high-risk, high-reward opportunities in early-stage projects. He chose three small-cap tokens that focused on real-world asset tokenization, decentralized shipping logistics, and AI on the blockchain. He knew these might fail — but if just one succeeded, it could shift his entire portfolio. This layer was his chance to break out of the paycheck-to-paycheck loop and build real leverage from insight.

Marcus also kept 10% in stablecoins — just in case. He knew he'd need the dry powder when markets dipped. When his first crypto winter hit, that stablecoin reserve saved him. While others panicked and sold at a loss, Marcus bought more of his core assets at a discount. His system worked — not because he was smarter, but because he was prepared.

To keep things disciplined, he set a monthly recurring investment of $300. Every payday, that amount was automatically transferred and deployed according to his portfolio structure. He stopped trying to time the market and instead focused on consistency. He reviewed his portfolio every three months, rebalanced when a token ballooned beyond its original percentage, and kept emotion out of it.

By the end of his second year, Marcus had contributed a total of $10,000. Thanks to some smart asymmetric wins and a strong bull run, his portfolio was worth just over $78,000. He was stunned. Not only had he outperformed his 401(k) — he had done it with a plan he built from scratch. A year later, after taking profits and compounding his gains through staking and yield farming, he crossed $125,000. A six-figure portfolio — built from patience, structure, and a willingness to learn.

Marcus's life changed, not just financially, but mentally. He saw the system differently. He no longer felt trapped by traditional finance. He had options. Confidence. Control. He used some profits to pay off debt, took his wife on a long-overdue vacation, and began saving for his daughter's college fund — in stablecoins and BTC.

When friends asked him how he did it, Marcus didn't point them to a meme coin or secret tip. He told them about portfolio layers. About understanding risk. About staying consistent when it was boring and brave when it was scary. And above all, about treating crypto like a long-term business, not a lottery ticket.

Marcus's story is not unique. It's the story of anyone who trades hype for structure and emotion for strategy. The six-figure blueprint isn't reserved for tech geniuses or Silicon Valley insiders. It's for anyone — anywhere — willing to learn, commit, and build over time. Like Marcus, you don't have to swing for the fences. You just have to show up, every month, with a plan.

Chapter 4: Navigating Bull and Bear Markets

If you want to build real wealth in the crypto economy, you must learn to master the cycles — especially the emotional rollercoaster of bull and bear markets. Most people are reactive. They buy high, sell low, and repeat the same mistakes every four years. But successful investors aren't victims of the cycle — they *use* it. They accumulate when others flee and harvest profits when euphoria blinds the herd. In this chapter, you'll learn how to build wealth in both bull and bear markets by recognizing patterns, setting rules, and sticking to strategy.

Let's start with bull markets — the part everyone loves. In crypto, bull markets are characterized by rapid price appreciation, mainstream media coverage, exploding user growth, and massive inflows of retail capital. During these periods, portfolio values can multiply fast — 2x, 5x, even 10x in a matter of months. But with that upside comes a major risk: *greed.* People start to believe the price will only go up. They overallocate. They ignore fundamentals. They stop taking profits.

A wealth builder uses bull markets not to *enter* — but to *exit.* That doesn't mean selling everything, but it does mean having a plan. One common method is a **tiered profit-taking**

strategy. For example, sell 20% of your position after a 3x gain, 20% more after a 5x, and another chunk after a 10x. This lets you ride the upside while locking in gains along the way. Another approach is to sell back your original investment after a major pump — allowing you to play with "house money" for the rest of the cycle. The key is to set these plans *before* the price takes off — not during.

Bull markets are also a time to **rotate capital**. As large-cap assets peak, capital often flows into mid- and low-cap coins. Timing these "altcoin seasons" can multiply your returns, but requires discipline. Chasing trends late in the cycle can lead to devastating drawdowns. That's why some investors use portfolio caps — for example, no more than 5% in any one micro-cap, or a maximum 20% exposure to experimental projects. As gains come in, reallocate into more stable assets like BTC, ETH, or stablecoins to protect your net worth.

Now let's turn to bear markets — the quiet, painful, and *critical* part of the cycle. This is when the tourists leave, prices collapse, and social media goes silent. But for wealth builders, bear markets are a gift. This is where you accumulate discounted assets, build conviction, and plant seeds for the next bull cycle. The problem is, most people are too scared to buy when prices fall 70% or more. They believe the market is dead. That's when opportunity is greatest.

In bear markets, the name of the game is **capital preservation and accumulation**. You should double down on your education, evaluate projects for long-term value, and keep DCAing into your high-conviction holdings. Your asymmetric bets can still exist, but you'll want to be even more selective and conservative. In many cases, it's better to increase your exposure to blue-chip assets like BTC and ETH — which tend to lead the recovery in each new cycle.

It's during bear markets that you build **mental resilience**. You'll question your decisions. You'll be tempted to sell it all. But remember: every bull run in history started in the ashes of a bear. If you capitulate at the bottom, you'll miss the next run entirely. That's why many long-term investors use **automatic investing plans** during bear seasons — setting fixed recurring buys regardless of market sentiment. This removes emotion from the equation and ensures you're always building your position when prices are low.

Bear markets are also a great time to **rebalance your portfolio**. Maybe your high-risk plays didn't perform. Maybe you overextended into NFTs or meme tokens. Now's the time to reflect, cut losers, and restructure for strength. Shift capital toward real infrastructure, cash-flowing DeFi protocols, or tokens with upcoming catalysts. Consolidate. Simplify. Reposition.

Whether in a bull or bear market, having a **cycle strategy** is essential. Many crypto veterans follow the "four-year Bitcoin cycle," which typically includes accumulation, breakout, mania, and collapse. Aligning your behavior with these phases can keep you focused and grounded. Accumulate before the halving. Take profits during euphoric runs. Exit speculative bets before the top. And during the crash — stay calm, stay educated, and rebuild.

Also, consider the **macro environment**. Global interest rates, inflation, regulations, and tech innovation all affect crypto markets. For instance, rising interest rates often reduce risk appetite across all asset classes, including crypto. Being aware of macro signals can help you anticipate market shifts and adjust your position sizes accordingly. Wealth builders study more than just charts — they study the world.

Finally, track your emotions. Greed and fear are always strongest when action is required most. During bull runs, when you feel invincible — that's when you need to take profits. During bear markets, when it feels hopeless — that's when you need to keep building. Set rules and automate decisions wherever possible. It's not about predicting the market perfectly — it's about removing emotion so you can execute your long-term plan.

The market will always move in cycles. But wealth isn't built in the peak — it's built in the valley. If you can master bull and bear markets, you won't just survive the crypto economy — you'll thrive in it. In the next chapter, we'll talk about protecting what you've built: wealth preservation, risk management, and intelligent exits.

Ava's trading experience

Ava sat at her kitchen table, staring at the green candles lighting up her portfolio. It was late 2021, and the crypto market was on fire. Ethereum had doubled in two months. Solana was making new all-time highs daily. Her small investment in a decentralized storage token had exploded 15x. Her phone buzzed constantly with alerts, Twitter was filled with euphoric predictions, and her friends — many of whom mocked her crypto investments a year earlier — were now begging for tips. She felt like a genius. But something didn't sit right.

Just a year earlier, Ava had been on the opposite end of the cycle. In early 2020, she had entered crypto cautiously — dollar-cost averaging into Bitcoin and Ethereum. By the time the pandemic crash hit, her portfolio was down 60%. The headlines screamed "Crypto Is Dead," and her confidence wavered. But instead of panicking, she went deeper. She studied market history. She discovered the concept of four-year cycles. She learned that bear markets weren't the end — they were the beginning of wealth-building. So, she did what few had the courage to do: she kept investing.

That experience burned something into her memory. So now, with her portfolio up more than 500% and growing fast, Ava remembered how quickly things could change. She re-read her notes, opened her original plan, and began taking profits. Not everything. Just 20% from each position that had doubled. She moved those profits into stablecoins and began looking for signs of euphoria: magazine covers, celebrity endorsements, friends with no investing experience suddenly giving crypto advice. It was all there. The cycle was peaking — and she knew it.

In the weeks that followed, the market soared even higher. Ava questioned her decision. She felt FOMO — fear of missing out — especially when a coin she sold continued to rise another 40%. But she stuck to her plan. And then, almost overnight, it happened. The crash. Bitcoin fell 30%. Then 50%. Altcoins dropped 70% or more. Social media went silent. Influencers disappeared. Ava watched her portfolio fall — but she wasn't afraid. She had stablecoins on the sidelines and had already locked in life-changing profits. She wasn't just surviving the crash — she was preparing for the next cycle.

During the bear market, Ava rebalanced. She cleaned out deadweight tokens, studied new protocols, and invested heavily in herself. While others walked away from crypto in frustration, she leaned in. She joined a DAO, started earning yield on her stablecoins, and doubled down on Bitcoin and Ethereum when prices hit multi-year lows. It wasn't exciting – but it was powerful. Ava understood that wealth was built in the shadows, not in the spotlight.

Two years later, as the market began to turn, Ava's preparation paid off again. Her reinvestments during the bear gave her a massive head start. While others were scrambling to catch up, she was already positioned. The new bull run hadn't even peaked, and she was back at all-time highs – with double the portfolio value she had at the last peak. But this time, she was calm. Confident. Strategic. She had mastered the cycles.

Ava's story is not about predicting the top or bottom perfectly. It's about having a plan and the emotional discipline to follow it. She used bull markets to take profits and rotate capital. She used bear markets to rebuild and accumulate. She didn't get caught in the crowd's hysteria. She listened to the market, followed her strategy, and made decisions from strength – not fear.

Crypto cycles will always repeat. Bull markets will seduce you. Bear markets will try to break you. But the people who understand the rhythm, who act with intention instead of emotion, will come out ahead. Like Ava, you don't have to be perfect — you just have to be prepared.

Chapter 5: Wealth Preservation and Exit Plans

Growing your crypto portfolio is only half the equation. The other half — often overlooked — is keeping it. Many investors focus solely on accumulation and moonshot gains but never learn how to *preserve* their wealth. That's why countless people go from six- or seven-figure portfolios back to zero in a single cycle. In this chapter, you'll learn how to protect your gains, reduce risk as you grow, and create an exit plan that helps you turn digital wealth into real-world security.

Wealth preservation starts with a simple principle: **you don't win until you exit**. A paper profit is just that — paper. Markets can reverse quickly, and without a plan, emotions can lead to poor decisions. That's why the first rule of wealth preservation is to define **when and how you'll take profits**. This doesn't mean selling everything at the top (an impossible task), but rather setting clear milestones. For example, you might choose to withdraw your initial capital after a 2x gain, take 25% off the table after a 5x, and another portion at a 10x. These predefined steps reduce the temptation to hold everything indefinitely.

Your **exit plan** should include multiple tiers: partial exits during bull markets, automatic rebalancing strategies, and conversion into safer assets like stablecoins or even fiat when appropriate. Many long-term crypto investors follow a "rotate and withdraw" strategy — taking profits from high-performing assets and reallocating them into cash-flowing DeFi protocols or blue-chip coins, or moving them entirely off-chain into real-world assets such as real estate or precious metals. This flow ensures that your gains serve a purpose beyond the portfolio screen.

Wealth preservation also requires **risk mitigation through diversification**. If your entire portfolio is riding on five highly volatile tokens, one major downturn can wipe out years of gains. A well-balanced portfolio should include a mix of long-term holds (BTC, ETH), mid-caps with utility, asymmetric bets, and stablecoins or hedged assets. As your portfolio grows, your risk tolerance should evolve — and your allocations should shift accordingly. The wealthier you become, the more of your portfolio should be focused on protecting that wealth rather than chasing the next 10x.

Another key strategy is using **cold storage**. If you're holding large amounts of crypto on centralized exchanges, you're vulnerable to hacks, fraud, or regulatory freezes. Use hardware wallets like Ledger or Trezor to store your long-term holdings offline, and only keep trading or yield-generating assets on hot wallets or exchanges. Ownership is everything in crypto — and self-custody is one of the most powerful tools for wealth preservation.

Don't forget about **tax implications**. In many jurisdictions, crypto gains are considered taxable events — especially when converting to fiat or using crypto for purchases. Smart investors track every trade, withdrawal, and wallet interaction using tools like Koinly or CoinTracking. Depending on your country, long-term holdings may receive more favorable tax treatment, and losses may be deductible. Ignoring taxes can turn your portfolio growth into a future liability, so make this part of your wealth protection strategy from day one.

In addition to exit planning and protection, wealth preservation means creating **off-ramps to the real world**. What will you *do* with your gains? Will you invest in real estate? Start a business? Pay off debt? Fund your retirement? The most powerful reason to exit isn't fear — it's purpose. When your crypto wealth is connected to meaningful life goals, you're more likely to act rationally and preserve your legacy.

One powerful tool for long-term wealth preservation is **stablecoin yield farming**. Once you've taken profits, you can park them in high-yield protocols that generate 5% to 15% annually — far better than traditional banks. Of course, you'll need to assess smart contract risk, platform stability, and liquidity constraints, but when done correctly, this turns your idle cash into a steady income stream. It's a way of letting your realized gains continue working while you wait for the next opportunity.

Finally, consider setting up **trusts, LLCs, or multisig wallets** if you're managing large portfolios. These structures offer legal protection, estate planning benefits, and added security. As your wealth grows, you'll want to think like a business — not just an individual. That includes succession planning, inheritance strategies, and protecting your family's financial future.

The goal of building wealth in crypto is not just to see numbers go up. It's to change your life. To have freedom. To create a cushion that protects you through economic downturns. To give, invest, and grow in ways you couldn't before. That requires discipline, foresight, and a willingness to act when the time comes. Don't be the person who watched their portfolio rise — and then fall — because they had no plan to exit.

In the next chapter, we'll explore how to use advanced tools — from on-chain analytics to portfolio trackers and yield optimizers — to manage your growing wealth and make smarter, faster, data-driven decisions.

Elias' real asset conversion plan

Elias had spent three years carefully growing his crypto portfolio. What started as a side interest during lockdown — learning about Bitcoin and Ethereum — had turned into a disciplined routine. Every Friday after work, he'd sit at his desk, open his spreadsheet, and review his investments. He wasn't a full-time trader, influencer, or coder. Just a regular 42-year-old father and small business owner in Texas who had discovered a quiet passion for building wealth in the digital economy.

By late 2022, Elias had grown his portfolio to just over $250,000. He had taken early positions in ETH, AVAX, and a gaming token that had skyrocketed during the last bull run. But this time, he didn't want to make the same mistake he saw so many others make — riding the high until it crashed. A year prior, he'd watched a friend build a seven-figure portfolio and lose nearly all of it by refusing to sell. It left a lasting impression. Elias was determined to do better. He knew that real wealth wasn't built on hype — it was *kept* through strategy.

He sat down and wrote his first official exit plan. His goal wasn't to cash out completely but to systematically pull profits, protect what he'd built, and convert some gains into tangible, life-enhancing assets. His first milestone was simple: when any asset doubled, he would withdraw his original investment. That way, he'd be "risk-free" on that position. If it grew beyond 5x, he would begin rotating part of the profits into stablecoins — specifically USDC and DAI — and move them into trusted DeFi protocols to earn yield while waiting for new opportunities.

Elias also wanted to take part of his portfolio off the digital grid. He sold a small portion of Bitcoin and used the proceeds to pay off a high-interest business loan. That single move gave him a psychological edge — for the first time, his crypto gains had directly improved his real-world financial security. It changed everything. His investments were no longer just numbers on a screen. They were freedom. Options. Leverage.

He began converting other wins into stablecoins and using them to earn passive income through staking and lending. He moved long-term holdings into cold storage using a hardware wallet, and he set up a second wallet with a multi-signature option for estate planning. His wife, previously skeptical of crypto, began asking questions — and eventually joined him in designing a family wealth preservation plan. They even sat down with a financial advisor to understand their local tax laws and how to reduce their future liability.

Elias also took a broader view. He created a "real asset conversion plan," where 20% of his future profits would go toward tangible assets: land, solar panels, and even a small rental property in his hometown. He knew crypto markets moved in cycles, and he didn't want to find himself rich in one season and broke in the next. His mindset had matured — from accumulator to protector. And that mindset made him unshakable.

So when the market cooled in early 2023 and many investors panicked, Elias felt calm. He had already taken profits. His core holdings were secured. His emergency fund was in stablecoins earning yield. And he had diversified into real-world income streams. Crypto was still part of his life, but it no longer consumed him. He didn't check prices daily. He had structure. A system. Peace.

Elias's story is a reminder that preservation is power. Building a six- or seven-figure portfolio means little if you have no plan to lock in gains or protect capital. But with discipline, intentionality, and a commitment to long-term thinking, crypto wealth can translate into lasting freedom. Real wealth isn't measured by how high your portfolio climbs — but by how much of it you keep when the market shifts.

Chapter 6: Advanced Tools for Wealth Builders

As your crypto portfolio grows, so should your toolset. Building wealth in the crypto economy is no longer just about buying and holding – it's about managing data, automating your strategy, minimizing risk, and making intelligent, informed decisions. Whether you're aiming to grow your portfolio from five to six figures or to protect a seven-figure stack, the right tools can give you a major edge. In this chapter, we'll walk through some of the most powerful platforms, apps, and dashboards used by modern crypto wealth builders.

Let's start with **portfolio trackers**, which are essential for visibility and control. Once you move beyond a few assets or wallets, manually updating spreadsheets becomes a nightmare. Apps like **CoinStats**, **Delta**, and **Zerion** allow you to link wallets, track performance in real-time, monitor gas fees, and even view historical profit/loss breakdowns. For serious investors, **Debank** and **Zapper** offer DeFi-specific dashboards that track your yield farming positions, staking balances, and lending activities across multiple protocols. These tools help you see your entire portfolio at a glance – across chains, tokens, and platforms – so you can rebalance with clarity.

Next up: **on-chain analytics tools**. These platforms let you look under the hood of the blockchain and identify trends before they become headlines. **Glassnode**, **CryptoQuant**, and **IntoTheBlock** provide metrics like active addresses, exchange inflows, HODL ratios, and whale activity. These insights allow you to spot accumulation trends, identify overbought/oversold conditions, and gauge overall market sentiment. For example, a spike in BTC exchange inflows might signal incoming sell pressure, while a rise in stablecoin supply on exchanges could signal fresh buying power. These tools help you act with data, not emotion.

For DeFi power users, **yield aggregators and optimizers** like **Yearn Finance**, **Beefy Finance**, or **Idle Finance** automate yield strategies across multiple protocols. These platforms help you maximize APY while minimizing active management. Some even auto-compound your rewards or move funds between protocols based on changing yield rates. While these tools often charge small performance fees, the automation they provide can significantly boost returns over time — especially for those who understand the underlying risks and mechanics.

When it comes to **tax tracking and compliance**, tools like **Koinly**, **CoinTracking.info**, and **TokenTax** are indispensable. These platforms track your transaction history across wallets and exchanges, calculate capital gains and losses, and generate tax reports based on your country's regulations. As your portfolio grows, the cost of getting your taxes wrong becomes too high to ignore. By syncing your wallets early and keeping your records clean, you avoid the headache of trying to backtrack months (or years) of activity when tax season arrives.

Security is also a major consideration. You'll want to use **multi-factor authentication apps** like **Authy** or **Google Authenticator**, password managers like **1Password**, and — most importantly — **hardware wallets** like **Ledger** or **Trezor** for cold storage. As a wealth builder, you're a target. Don't store large sums on centralized exchanges. Use **multisig wallets** like **Gnosis Safe** if you're managing community or business funds, and enable **passphrase protection** on your cold wallet to add an extra layer of security. One breach could undo years of compounding. Treat security as part of your wealth strategy — because it is.

For research and discovery, platforms like **Token Terminal**, **Messari**, and **Dune Analytics** provide deep insights into token performance, protocol revenue, and user adoption trends. These tools allow you to filter the noise and focus on fundamentals. If you're serious about asymmetric investing, you can use **Dune** to build custom dashboards and track metrics unique to your investment thesis — such as NFT trading volume, DAO treasury balances, or Layer 2 adoption curves.

You'll also want to monitor **market sentiment** with tools like the **Fear & Greed Index**, **Santiment**, and **LunarCrush**, which analyze social media trends, developer activity, and community engagement. When sentiment is at peak fear, it may be a signal to accumulate. When greed takes over and everyone believes the market can't fall — it usually does. These signals aren't perfect, but they help guide contrarian thinking, which is often where the biggest wealth opportunities exist.

For automating execution, **trading bots** and **automation platforms** like **3Commas**, **Shrimpy**, and **Stoic** can help you set up automated DCA, rebalancing, and take-profit strategies. Even if you don't actively trade, automating small recurring tasks reduces decision fatigue and improves consistency. You can also use **IFTTT** or **Zapier** to set up crypto-related alerts, track news headlines, or trigger backup processes based on portfolio changes.

Finally, build a **crypto dashboard or command center** — a simple Notion, Google Sheet, or custom workspace that gives you a central place to track your portfolio, key news links, tax deadlines, investment rules, and goal milestones. Treat your wealth like a business. If you're serious about turning crypto into freedom, you need a control center to manage it all — not a collection of bookmarks and screenshots.

To sum up, tools don't build wealth — but they *amplify* it. They reduce mistakes. They provide clarity. They help you act faster, smarter, and with more confidence. The goal is not to use every tool available — it's to find the ones that fit your strategy and scale your edge. Because in crypto, *knowledge plus leverage equals power*. And the right tools give you both.

In the next chapter, we'll explore real-world case studies of people who used these tools and strategies to go from modest investments to six- and seven-figure portfolios — and the lessons we can learn from their journeys.

Rina. The non-techie

Rina was never much of a tech person. A former schoolteacher from New Zealand, she stumbled into crypto through a friend who gifted her a small amount of Ethereum as a thank-you. Curious, she started learning the basics. At first, she scribbled wallet addresses in a notebook and used sticky notes to track her holdings. But as her portfolio grew and she began dabbling in DeFi, she quickly realized that her system — or lack thereof — wasn't going to cut it.

One day, after missing out on a high-yield opportunity because she couldn't move funds in time, she decided to get organized. That evening, she discovered CoinStats — a sleek app that connected to her wallets and let her see her entire portfolio in one view. For the first time, she could track her performance, watch her profit and loss in real-time, and even get alerts for price changes. It felt like stepping out of the dark.

As Rina's curiosity deepened, so did her confidence. She started using DeBank and Zapper to monitor her positions across multiple chains — Ethereum, Polygon, Arbitrum. She discovered that she had forgotten funds sitting in a yield farm she'd joined months earlier. That tiny amount had nearly doubled thanks to compounding — and she'd almost lost it simply by forgetting it existed. From that point on, she committed to using dashboards not just as a convenience but as a wealth management necessity.

To make better decisions, Rina began studying on-chain analytics. She learned to read exchange inflows on CryptoQuant, analyzed wallet activity with Glassnode, and used IntoTheBlock to understand when whales were accumulating. It was empowering — like being able to see the moves of smart money in real time. While others were guessing, Rina was using data. That gave her clarity during crashes and confidence during dips. She wasn't just reacting anymore — she was preparing.

When it came to taxes, Rina realized she needed help. A few trades here and there had turned into dozens of transactions across multiple wallets and exchanges. She signed up for Koinly, synced her wallets, and immediately saw how much easier things could be. The software categorized her gains, flagged taxable events, and even provided the exact report her accountant needed. What would have taken days of manual work was now done in minutes. That tax report saved her thousands in avoidable penalties — and gave her peace of mind.

Security became another priority. Rina had heard horror stories of exchange hacks and phishing scams. She bought a Ledger hardware wallet, transferred her long-term holdings, and began using Google Authenticator for all logins. She also installed a password manager and learned how to set up multisig wallets for added protection. As her wealth grew, so did her awareness — and her sense of responsibility.

Rina even created her own Notion dashboard — a simple page where she kept track of her crypto goals, links to favorite tools, weekly tasks, and performance metrics. Every Sunday, she'd pour a cup of tea and run through her system: check her rebalancing sheet, review her staking rewards, read through Token Terminal for protocol revenue insights, and adjust her asymmetric bets accordingly. It became her version of a personal finance boardroom — a quiet, structured ritual that kept her grounded.

Now, with her portfolio approaching six figures, Rina credits her success not to any one token or bull market — but to her system. Her tools didn't just help her grow her wealth — they helped her *keep* it. They gave her visibility, control, and clarity. And in a market that moves faster than any other in the world, those three things are priceless.

Rina's journey is proof that wealth-building in crypto doesn't require complexity — it requires commitment. Tools aren't a luxury. They're a foundation. Whether you're a beginner with $500 or a seasoned investor with $500,000, the right tools create structure, eliminate emotion, and unlock potential you didn't even know you had.

Chapter 7: Case Studies — From $5K to $500K+

Reading strategies and frameworks is important — but *seeing* them applied in real life can be even more powerful. In this chapter, we'll explore several real-world case studies of individuals who used the principles we've discussed to grow modest crypto investments into six- and seven-figure portfolios. These examples are not about hype or luck. They're about discipline, conviction, asymmetric thinking, and smart decisions made consistently. Whether you're starting with $500 or $50,000, the lessons from these stories are universally applicable.

Let's begin with **Case Study 1: The Accumulator**. David was a 29-year-old accountant in California who started investing in crypto during the 2018 bear market. He didn't try to time the bottom — instead, he committed to investing $250 per month, regardless of price. Over the course of three years, he built positions in Bitcoin, Ethereum, and a handful of DeFi tokens. During the 2021 bull run, those disciplined monthly investments — totaling around $9,000 — grew to nearly $140,000. His biggest wins were not from high-risk tokens, but from holding and compounding blue-chip assets over time. His success shows that time in the market beats timing the market — especially when you remove emotion from the equation.

Case Study 2: The Asymmetric Thinker focuses on Jamila, a software developer in Kenya who started with just $1,000. She studied tokenomics, followed developer activity on GitHub, and invested early in a decentralized freelance platform aimed at emerging markets. Her $200 position in that token eventually grew to over $30,000 when adoption soared during a global remote work surge. She only needed one win — supported by a real use case and research — to multiply her portfolio. Jamila's story emphasizes the power of asymmetric bets, especially for investors outside traditional financial hubs who understand local problems better than anyone else.

Then we have **Case Study 3: The Cycle Strategist**, Michael — a 41-year-old real estate agent in Canada. He started with $5,000 and scaled to $80,000 over a few years using strict cycle analysis. He studied Bitcoin halving events, tracked sentiment, and rotated profits during bull markets into stablecoins. During the 2022 bear market, he deployed those stablecoins into ETH and MATIC near cycle lows. When prices recovered, his portfolio passed $250,000. His secret? Not reacting emotionally. He treated crypto like a seasonal business and planned his moves like a chess player. His story proves that awareness of cycles — and disciplined action — is a true edge.

Case Study 4: The Yield Farmer, Natalia from Spain, illustrates the power of passive compounding. She began with $20,000 and focused exclusively on yield-generating DeFi protocols. She learned to assess smart contract risk, chose stablecoins during volatile seasons, and optimized returns through auto-compounding vaults on Yearn and Beefy. Over two years, her average return was around 18% annually — but when the bull cycle kicked in and she rotated into high-yield governance tokens at the right moment, her portfolio ballooned to over $220,000. Natalia shows that patient, low-drama investing works — especially when paired with strategic timing.

Case Study 5: The Exit Architect is about Andre, a Brazilian entrepreneur who grew his crypto stack from $15,000 to nearly $500,000 by the peak of the bull market. Unlike many others, he didn't get greedy. He had a detailed exit strategy: selling in tranches at 2x, 5x, and 10x milestones. He moved profits into real estate and even bought a small eco-farm near São Paulo. When the market crashed in 2022, he had already locked in his gains and was earning income from his physical assets. His remaining crypto holdings were in cold storage, and he used stablecoin yield to supplement cash flow. Andre's story reinforces that wealth is *realized* when you take action — not just when it appears on your screen.

Across these examples, several common themes emerge:

- **Discipline beats emotion**. Every successful investor had a written plan, automated their investing or exits, and stayed consistent.
- **Asymmetry is real**. Small, researched positions in high-upside projects changed lives — but none of the individuals went "all in" recklessly.
- **Cycles matter**. Timing matters less than structure — but those who recognized macro trends and acted accordingly grew faster with less risk.
- **Wealth is preserved, not just earned**. Whether through real estate, cash-flow strategies, or cold storage, every case study involved protecting gains.
- **Tools were essential**. Each person used some form of tracker, analytics, or automation to manage complexity and maintain control.

The takeaway is clear: anyone — regardless of background, income, or geography — can grow life-changing wealth through crypto with the right mindset, structure, and behavior.

You don't need to be perfect. You don't need to time the market. But you do need a system, a plan, and the ability to think independently.

In the next chapter, we'll look into the **future of wealth in Web3** — including DAOs, tokenized real estate, and the emerging financial rails of tomorrow's economy. Because the next wave of opportunity is already forming — and it will reward those who are ready.

Amir's story

When Amir first started exploring crypto, he had just been laid off from his job in hospitality during the early pandemic shutdowns. With a severance check of $6,000 and no immediate opportunities on the horizon, he could have played it safe — hoarding cash, cutting expenses, and hoping something would come along. Instead, Amir chose to take a calculated risk. He invested $1,000 into Bitcoin and Ethereum, not expecting to become rich overnight, but determined to learn everything he could about this new financial frontier.

He read voraciously. Whitepapers, podcasts, YouTube deep-dives, Twitter threads — anything he could get his hands on. He learned about halving cycles, smart contracts, gas fees, and tokenomics. But most importantly, he learned about *conviction*. When the market dipped 20%, then 40%, Amir didn't sell. He kept contributing small amounts each month, treating his crypto portfolio like a business. Within two years, that $1,000 had become over $40,000. And by the time the next bull run arrived, his consistent strategy had ballooned his portfolio past $120,000. Amir hadn't chased hype — he built his wealth through patience and discipline.

Across the world in the Philippines, Dana had a different story. A freelance virtual assistant supporting Western clients, she had limited access to traditional investing tools. But she *did* have internet, curiosity, and a knack for spotting overlooked opportunities. When she heard about a new token designed to streamline payments for freelancers in Southeast Asia, she took a chance. She invested just $300 — what she'd normally earn in a week. Over the next six months, that token exploded. It landed listings on major exchanges and was adopted by several platforms she herself used for work. Her $300 turned into $25,000. But Dana didn't get greedy. She sold half, paid off family debts, and used the rest to fund an online course on blockchain marketing — which helped her 3x her freelance rates.

Then there was Jordan, a small-town gym owner in Ohio. He was skeptical of crypto at first, but after a client gifted him a $50 hardware wallet with a bit of Bitcoin on it, he got curious. He started watching market cycles and discovered that most people lost money by entering during peaks and panicking during dips. So Jordan made a plan: he would DCA into BTC and ETH every month, without fail, and avoid hype coins altogether. Three years later, his $5,000 in total contributions had grown to over $80,000. He used a portion of it to renovate his gym and reinvested the rest into real estate. Crypto didn't just boost his portfolio — it rebuilt his business.

In Brazil, Luciana was an early adopter of DeFi. She wasn't a coder, but she was resourceful. She started yield farming with stablecoins during the bear market when most people had written off crypto. By using automated vaults and conservative strategies, she generated 10–15% annual returns on capital she'd already pulled from other investments. Over time, her $20,000 grew quietly and steadily. Then, when the bull market returned, she rotated into governance tokens of the very protocols she'd been using. Some of those 10x'd. Luciana's portfolio hit $230,000 — not from speculation, but from participation, strategy, and compounding.

And finally, there was Leandro, an investor in Argentina who saw crypto as a hedge against inflation. He lived through financial instability and currency devaluation, so digital assets weren't just an opportunity — they were a necessity. Leandro focused on fundamentals: blue-chip assets, diversified stablecoin reserves, and real-world asset tokenization. As his portfolio crossed six figures, he used profits to buy land, build a small guesthouse, and install solar panels. He wasn't looking to flash wealth. He was building *resilience*. Crypto gave him the tools to create a sustainable life — not just a rich one.

Each of these stories is different — but they all echo the same truths: start where you are, invest with intention, and think long-term. Crypto rewards consistency, conviction, and creativity. You don't need millions to begin. You need a system, a plan, and the willingness to stay the course.

The path from $5K to $500K isn't paved in luck. It's built with small, smart decisions that compound over time. The next story could be yours.

Chapter 8: The Future of Wealth in Web3

As powerful as crypto has been over the past decade, the real transformation is just beginning. The next phase of the digital economy is Web3 — a new internet architecture that shifts ownership, governance, and value exchange into the hands of users. For crypto wealth builders, understanding where Web3 is headed isn't just about staying current — it's about positioning for the *next wave* of opportunity. In this chapter, we'll explore how wealth creation will evolve in the Web3 era, including DAOs, tokenized real-world assets, decentralized identity, and new income models based on participation.

At its core, **Web3** represents a shift from platforms to protocols, from users to owners. In Web2, you contribute content, data, and time — but you own nothing. In Web3, your participation is rewarded with tokens, NFTs, or shares in the network itself. This changes everything. It turns consumers into stakeholders. It turns social networks, marketplaces, and even video games into *economies*. And for investors who can spot early adoption, Web3 creates asymmetric opportunities far beyond what we've seen before.

One of the most exciting wealth-building vehicles in Web3 is the **DAO** — Decentralized Autonomous Organization. These are internet-native entities governed by smart contracts and token holders instead of traditional executives or boards. DAOs can be investment clubs, grant-giving bodies, service providers, or even full-scale businesses. As a crypto investor, participating in DAOs offers three distinct benefits: early access to promising projects, voting rights over treasury allocations, and potential token rewards or dividends from DAO activities. Some DAOs even pay contributors in stablecoins or governance tokens. The key to benefiting is not just buying DAO tokens — it's *participating*, helping to shape the future of the organization you believe in.

Another key development in Web3 is the rise of **tokenized real-world assets (RWAs)**. These are physical or off-chain assets like real estate, carbon credits, treasury bills, or fine art, represented as blockchain-based tokens. Tokenization unlocks liquidity in traditionally illiquid markets and allows fractional ownership and 24/7 trading. Platforms like Goldfinch, Centrifuge, and RealT are pioneering these models. For investors, RWAs represent a bridge between crypto and traditional finance — providing stable yield with on-chain transparency. Imagine earning 8% on tokenized commercial real estate, without needing to be a millionaire or jumping through institutional hoops.

Decentralized identity (DID) is another frontier. In Web3, your wallet becomes your passport. Your on-chain history, NFTs, DAO memberships, and even credentials from learning platforms can form a reputation layer that replaces usernames and passwords. Projects like ENS (Ethereum Name Service), Lens Protocol, and Soulbound Tokens are exploring this space. As identity moves on-chain, new wealth models will emerge – from reputation-based lending to verified access for premium content or services. Owning identity infrastructure or investing in early DID ecosystems could become as important as owning real estate in the early internet.

Web3 also introduces **new income models** that reward contribution instead of extraction. Imagine being paid for curating content, voting in governance, providing data, or even just showing up. Platforms like Mirror (for writing), Audius (for music), and Play-to-Earn ecosystems have already demonstrated this. But the real wealth may come not from being a user – but from owning the infrastructure that powers these systems. Investing early in creator-centric platforms, content protocols, and royalty-sharing tokens can unlock recurring income and equity-like upside.

Social tokens and community coins are another trend that will reshape personal brands and micro-economies. Influencers, educators, athletes, and entrepreneurs can launch tokens that represent access, loyalty, and value. These tokens can be tied to exclusive content, governance over a community treasury, or even long-term profit sharing. For investors, this means the chance to back communities — not just companies — and to benefit when those communities grow in strength and influence.

Another massive area is **modular finance** — the unbundling and re-bundling of financial products through composable smart contracts. Instead of relying on a single bank, users can stack protocols together: one for lending, one for collateralization, one for insurance, and one for payments. Investors who understand how these layers interact can identify the building blocks of the next great financial apps — and position themselves early. Yield strategies will no longer just rely on farming — they'll involve "money legos" and permissionless innovation.

In Web3, even **labor markets will evolve**. Instead of centralized freelancing platforms taking huge fees, protocols will allow direct connections, crypto payment streams, and credential verification. Projects like Braintrust, Superfluid, and Talent Protocol hint at this future. If you build or invest in these networks early, you'll gain exposure not just to financial returns, but to *ownership of economic infrastructure*.

Finally, it's worth understanding the **philosophy of**

abundance behind Web3. Unlike traditional finance, which often locks opportunity behind credentials or capital, Web3 is about *access*. Permissionless networks allow people from anywhere — regardless of status — to participate in value creation. This global inclusivity isn't just moral — it's profitable. The next 100 million Web3 users won't be from Silicon Valley. They'll be from Nigeria, Colombia, India, the Philippines — and they'll bring new use cases, talent, and ideas that drive growth.

As a wealth builder, your edge in Web3 won't just come from picking the right coin. It will come from *understanding the network effects of ownership*. From DAOs to decentralized data, from tokenized assets to participation-based income — Web3 gives you a front-row seat to the future of value.

In the next chapter, we'll explore how to take your Web3 knowledge global — by understanding crypto adoption in emerging markets, the barriers to access, and the immense opportunity ahead for those who can serve underbanked populations with decentralized tools.

Kai and Web3

Kai had always been fascinated by the internet. Growing up in South Korea, he built his first website at 12 and started a small gaming community by 15. But it wasn't until he discovered

Web3 in his mid-twenties that everything clicked. For the first time, he saw the internet not just as a place to consume and connect — but as a place to *own*. And with that realization, he began building not just digital projects — but digital *wealth*.

At first, Kai bought tokens like everyone else. But what caught his attention wasn't the prices — it was the *networks*. He joined a DAO focused on digital identity, where every contributor had voting rights over treasury decisions. Instead of being a customer, he was now a stakeholder. He helped write documentation, participated in governance calls, and was rewarded with tokens that grew in value as the protocol gained traction. His wallet became more than storage — it became his resume, proof of his contributions and his growing on-chain reputation.

As the months went by, Kai explored the world of tokenized real estate. He bought fractional ownership in a Miami condo through a platform called RealT, earning rent payments directly into his wallet in USDC. It was a lightbulb moment. For the first time, cross-border investment was seamless, permissionless, and efficient. He no longer needed to trust a middleman. His token *was* the deed. This wasn't speculation — it was income. And it taught him that Web3 wasn't just about crypto — it was about transforming how we own and manage everything.

He also discovered the power of decentralized identity. With his ENS name, his GitHub profile, and his DAO credentials linked to a single wallet, he began to get invited to gated events, whitelist opportunities, and even job offers — all based on his on-chain activity. He didn't need to submit a resume. His work spoke for itself. He realized that in Web3, your wallet could *become* your reputation — and that identity would be the foundation of future wealth-building.

Kai began experimenting with social tokens. He launched a small community coin for his newsletter subscribers. The token didn't just represent access — it gave holders a say in which topics he'd cover, and even revenue sharing from premium courses he was launching. As his audience grew, so did the value of the token. It was no longer about selling content — it was about co-creating an economy with his most loyal followers. This model, he realized, was the future for creators, teachers, and entrepreneurs alike.

But it wasn't all glamour. Kai learned about smart contract risk the hard way when a small DeFi protocol he was farming collapsed due to a bug. He lost $3,000 overnight. Instead of quitting, he doubled down on learning — how to audit code, how to evaluate protocol risk, and how to use tools like DeBank, Dune, and Snapshot to stay ahead. His losses became tuition. And his growth became exponential.

As he gained confidence, Kai began consulting with startups across Southeast Asia, helping them integrate Web3 tools into their platforms — loyalty points, NFT memberships, and DAO-style governance. He earned not in fiat, but in equity tokens. Some projects flopped. But one, a decentralized learning platform, took off. His small stake multiplied 40x in a year. It wasn't luck. It was his sweat equity — proof that in Web3, *builders are the new investors.*

Kai's story is still being written. But one thing is clear — he's not just investing in tokens. He's investing in infrastructure. In ownership. In the systems that will define the next era of the internet. He's not trying to get rich off the next meme coin. He's playing the long game — the one where wealth is built by helping create the networks we'll all use tomorrow.

The Web3 future belongs to those who *build and belong.* Whether it's through DAOs, decentralized ID, tokenized assets, or creator economies — the new rules of wealth are already here. And they don't require permission.

Chapter 9: Crypto Wealth and Global Opportunity

The crypto revolution isn't just a Silicon Valley story – it's a *global* one. While the spotlight often shines on Western investors and institutions, the real growth, adoption, and opportunity are exploding in emerging markets. From Nigeria to Argentina, the Philippines to Turkey, people are turning to crypto not as a speculative asset, but as a lifeline. For investors and builders alike, this chapter explores the massive potential of *global crypto adoption* and how it presents one of the most powerful, overlooked wealth opportunities of our time.

Let's start with the *why*. In many countries, inflation is out of control, banking systems are inefficient, and access to basic financial services is limited. Crypto offers a solution – decentralized, borderless, permissionless money. It enables people to store value in stablecoins rather than rapidly devaluing local currencies. It gives freelancers the ability to get paid instantly in USDC without high fees or bureaucratic red tape. It allows families to move money across borders in minutes, not days – and for a fraction of the cost. In short, crypto is solving *real problems*, and demand is rising fast.

Countries like **Argentina**, where inflation has surpassed 100%, have seen record growth in crypto usage. In **Nigeria**, peer-to-peer crypto trading volume ranks among the highest globally. **Turkey**, **Vietnam**, **India**, and **Ukraine** are all in the top 10 for adoption according to Chainalysis reports. These users aren't trading meme coins — they're using crypto for *survival, remittances, savings,* and *payments.* This is where the next wave of innovation and capital will be focused — and smart investors will be early.

As an investor, understanding global crypto adoption helps you identify *asymmetric opportunities* that others miss. For example, tokens focused on mobile-first DeFi, off-ramp infrastructure, micro-payments, or stablecoin usage in underbanked markets may seem "boring" to Western traders — but they're the beating heart of crypto in developing economies. Protocols like **Celo**, **Near**, **Reserve**, **World Mobile**, and **Valora** are building specifically for these users — often with smaller market caps and significant room to grow.

Investing in **localized platforms** — exchanges, wallets, and payment rails built for specific regions — can also lead to massive upside. Binance's expansion in Africa, Latin America, and Southeast Asia was a strategic bet on user growth, and newer players are following suit. If you're early to a project building crypto rails for rural India or North Africa, the return potential can be enormous — especially if that project gains government partnerships, NGO integrations, or mobile carrier support.

Beyond investing, there's another opportunity: *serving these markets.* Wealth builders who launch education products, tools, or services tailored to emerging markets can tap into billions of underserved users. Consider crypto courses in native languages, DeFi wallets with ultra-low fees, or NFT platforms focused on local art and culture. The people who solve *real problems* for real people — not just for early adopters in the West — will create businesses with global scale.

One key trend is the rise of **crypto-native employment**. As blockchain becomes global, so do job opportunities. Developers in Venezuela, designers in Ghana, marketers in Bangladesh — all are earning in crypto, joining DAOs, and freelancing for Web3 startups. Platforms like Gitcoin, Braintrust, and Dework allow workers in low-income countries to earn stablecoins or tokens, build on-chain reputations, and unlock financial freedom. As an investor or builder, helping scale these platforms or even launching one for a niche vertical could be immensely profitable — and impactful.

We also need to consider **stablecoins** as the backbone of global crypto wealth. For billions of people, the U.S. dollar — not Bitcoin — is the store of value they trust most. Stablecoins like USDC, USDT, and even algorithmic alternatives are becoming everyday money in places where banks fail. Projects building local stablecoin pairs, regional liquidity pools, or fiat-to-crypto bridges will play a key role in global adoption. Supporting these infrastructure layers today can lead to long-term wealth tomorrow.

Of course, there are challenges. Many emerging markets face regulatory uncertainty, internet connectivity issues, and local opposition. But the demand is already there. The need is real. And crypto, unlike traditional finance, doesn't wait for permission. Mobile wallets, peer-to-peer trading apps, and low-bandwidth DeFi protocols are already filling the gap. Builders and investors who anticipate these needs — and localize their solutions — will win.

Finally, global adoption is about **mindset**. If you're building wealth in crypto, you must think beyond your country, beyond your currency, beyond your limitations. The internet made knowledge global. Crypto makes value global. If you can see the patterns, identify the underserved, and align with mission-driven innovation, you won't just grow your portfolio — you'll help shape the financial future for billions.

In the next chapter — our final one — we'll help you create your **personal 5-year plan**, combining everything you've learned into a blueprint for sustainable crypto wealth. You've seen the strategies. You've met the builders. Now it's time to put it all together.

How Zuri went global

Zuri lived in Lagos, Nigeria — a city bursting with creativity, commerce, and contradictions. Her family had always struggled with currency volatility, inflation, and limited banking access. Getting paid as a remote worker was a challenge. Moving money across borders was expensive. And saving money? That was a battle against time. But everything changed when she discovered crypto — not as an investment trend, but as a tool for survival.

It started with a stablecoin. A client in the U.S. offered to pay her in USDC instead of her local currency. At first, she hesitated. But after a bit of research, she downloaded a wallet, received her first payment, and watched it settle in seconds — with zero fees. For the first time, Zuri didn't need to rely on the fragile banking infrastructure that had failed her so many times. Her money was now faster, safer, and worth more tomorrow than it was today.

Soon, she was telling friends and family. Her cousin used crypto to send money home from Europe without the steep remittance fees. Her friend from school began earning through

DAO gigs and receiving payments in stablecoins. They weren't trading meme coins — they were using crypto to build a better life.

Inspired, Zuri began learning about decentralized finance. She staked some USDC and earned interest. She explored yield farming and discovered ways to earn from protocols designed for mobile users in Africa. She saw projects like Celo and Valora building specifically for people like her — those who had skipped laptops and gone straight to phones. She felt seen.

She wasn't alone. In her online groups, she connected with people from Argentina, Vietnam, and Lebanon — all dealing with unstable economies but finding hope in blockchain. One Venezuelan artist sold NFT art and used the profits to feed his family. A woman in the Philippines earned crypto teaching English in a decentralized learning DAO. They weren't just surviving — they were *thriving*.

Zuri realized the crypto revolution wasn't happening in the headlines — it was happening in WhatsApp groups, Discord communities, and peer-to-peer apps in places the media rarely covered. It wasn't about Lambos and luxury — it was about dignity and independence. It was about mothers securing savings. Entrepreneurs raising capital. Teens building online empires from places that had been shut out of the financial system.

Eventually, Zuri launched her own business — a crypto onboarding service for local freelancers and small businesses. She taught people how to accept stablecoins, protect their wallets, and use DeFi to save and grow their earnings. She earned in crypto. She saved in crypto. She taught in crypto. And for the first time in her life, she wasn't afraid of her economy's next collapse. She was ready.

By the time global investors started paying attention to Africa's crypto boom, Zuri was already building with the best of them. Not only had she created financial security for herself, but she had helped hundreds of others do the same. And she did it without permission. Without venture capital. Without waiting for policy to catch up.

Zuri's story is one of millions — stories that won't make headlines but are reshaping the financial future from the ground up. While others debate crypto's legitimacy, the rest of the world is already using it. And as wealth builders, the lesson is clear: the greatest opportunities won't come from watching Wall Street. They'll come from watching the world.

Chapter 10: Putting It All Together — Your 5-Year Plan

By now, you've learned the core strategies of building wealth in the crypto economy — asymmetric investing, cycle mastery, risk management, smart exits, global opportunities, and the power of Web3 participation. But knowledge without a plan is potential wasted. In this final chapter, we'll bring everything together into a simple, powerful **5-year blueprint** to help you build, preserve, and scale a six- or seven-figure crypto portfolio with clarity and confidence.

Step 1: Define Your Wealth Goals

Before choosing tokens or strategies, define what wealth means to *you*. Is it a number? A lifestyle? Freedom from a job? Owning land? Supporting your family? Build around purpose — not hype. Your 5-year plan should reflect clear, measurable goals. For example:

- Reach a $250,000 net crypto portfolio
- Generate $2,000/month in passive crypto income
- Use profits to buy a debt-free home or property
- Fund early retirement or education expenses

Tie your crypto goals to real-world outcomes. This gives your plan gravity and motivation – especially during volatile seasons.

Step 2: Build Your Portfolio Structure

Your crypto wealth journey starts with **structure** – not just speculation. Use the layered approach:

- **40–60% Core Holdings**: Bitcoin, Ethereum, or other blue-chip assets
- **20–30% Mid-Caps**: Layer 1s, DeFi protocols, infrastructure tokens
- **10–20% Asymmetric Bets**: Small caps with huge upside potential
- **5–15% Stablecoins**: Dry powder for dips or stable yield

Rebalance every 3–6 months to lock in gains, reduce risk, and keep alignment with your goals. Think like an architect, not a gambler.

Step 3: Use Dollar-Cost Averaging + Cycles

Set up **automatic contributions** to your portfolio monthly or biweekly. This smooths out volatility and removes emotion. Combine DCA with **cycle awareness**:

- Accumulate during bear markets
- Take profits during parabolic moves
- Hold cash in late-stage bull runs
- Rotate back in during crashes

You won't time perfectly, and you don't have to. Just build a rhythm that lets you buy low, ride growth, and protect when it peaks.

Step 4: Automate, Track, and Analyze

Use tools to reduce stress and increase clarity:

- **Trackers**: CoinStats, Delta, Debank for portfolio visibility
- **Analytics**: Glassnode, Dune, CryptoQuant for market signals
- **Security**: Hardware wallets, MFA, multisig for protection

- **Tax Software**: Koinly, CoinTracking for compliance
- **Dashboards**: Notion, Google Sheets, or your own Command Center

Update your dashboard monthly. Review performance, rebalance as needed, and note learnings from each market cycle.

Step 5: Protect and Preserve

As your portfolio grows, *shift from growth to preservation.* That means:

- Moving profits into real-world assets (property, business, metals)
- Earning passive income from staking or yield farming
- Using cold storage for long-term holds
- Having a clear, written exit strategy
- Considering trusts, LLCs, or multisig wallets for estate planning

Wealth is not just about making — it's about keeping. Protect your wins like your future depends on it — because it does.

Step 6: Go Global and Participate

Web3 is global. Wealth creation doesn't just come from trading — it comes from *participation*. Choose one of the following:

- Join a DAO and contribute
- Launch a social token or NFT collection
- Build content on Web3 platforms like Mirror or Lens
- Invest in projects targeting emerging markets
- Learn to earn in a crypto-native job or gig economy

Each activity compounds your network, your skillset, and your on-chain reputation — all of which will pay dividends in the next cycle.

Step 7: Review Yearly and Evolve

At the end of each year, ask:

- What worked? What didn't?
- How did my net worth change?
- What lessons did I learn from the market?
- How can I adjust my allocations or risk profile?

- What new trends or narratives am I watching?

Your 5-year plan is not a rigid map. It's a living strategy — one that adapts with you and the evolving crypto ecosystem.

Sample Year-by-Year Milestones

Year 1: Build portfolio structure, automate DCA, join one DAO or Web3 community, reach \$10K–\$25K in crypto holdings **Year 2**: Add asymmetric plays, begin earning passive income, build an exit strategy, reach \$50K portfolio value **Year 3**: Take first profits, reinvest in real-world assets or yield, grow stablecoin reserves, contribute to one on-chain project **Year 4**: Cross six figures, diversify income with education, consulting, or social tokens, prepare for market rotation **Year 5**: Harvest gains, lock in long-term financial security, help others, and start the next wave of compounding

This plan is a blueprint — but the work is yours. You don't have to rush. You don't have to be perfect. You just have to *show up consistently* with intention, intelligence, and resilience.

In crypto, the future doesn't belong to the fastest. It belongs to those who think long-term, execute with purpose, and know when to protect what they've built.

You are one decision away from that journey. Make it count.

Now, let's go over Aarav's story

Aarav stood at the edge of a quiet beach in Goa, India, watching the sunrise with a sense of peace he hadn't felt in years. Just five years earlier, he had been stuck in a corporate IT job, commuting through chaos, saving what little he could, and wondering if financial freedom was just a myth for people born with advantages he didn't have. Then he discovered crypto. It started as curiosity — turned into commitment — and ultimately, into control over his life and future.

At the beginning, Aarav didn't know where to start. He didn't have a finance degree or tech connections. But he had a clear goal: to break free from the system that kept him grinding, to build enough wealth to choose how he lived, and to help others around him do the same. He wrote down his goal: "In 5 years, I will build a $250,000 crypto portfolio that pays me $2,000/month in passive income. I'll be debt-free, location-independent, and building things I love."

He started with $2,000 and a spreadsheet. He allocated 50% to Bitcoin and Ethereum, 30% to projects like Avalanche and Aave, and 10% to small, promising tokens solving real-world problems. The remaining 10%? Stablecoins — his safety net. He set up automatic monthly buys and began tracking his net worth every 30 days, regardless of price swings. His rule was simple: *be boring when others are loud, and be brave when others are silent.*

During the first year, his portfolio dipped. Then it soared. Then it dipped again. But he stuck to the plan — not because he was fearless, but because he had structure. He automated decisions. He updated his dashboard every Sunday. He reviewed his cycle notes. And slowly, something powerful happened: he stopped chasing trends and started anticipating them.

By the end of year two, he had taken his first small profits. He paid off a credit card. Bought his parents a new appliance. It wasn't glamorous — but it was progress. In year three, he rotated from parabolic tokens into stablecoin yield protocols and moved a chunk of capital into a tokenized rental property that paid him in USDC monthly. In year four, he helped a local NGO set up a donation system through crypto, offering to match their first $1,000. He was no longer just an investor. He was a builder. A contributor. A leader.

Now in year five, Aarav's portfolio has crossed $310,000. His passive income averages $2,200/month — enough to cover his life in Goa, invest in new projects, and even fund a startup idea with friends. But more importantly, he has *freedom*. The freedom to choose when he works. Who he works with. And why.

His five-year journey wasn't perfect. He missed some gains. Lost money on bad plays. Even got scammed once. But his system protected him. His mindset kept him grounded. And his purpose gave him something money couldn't buy: peace.

Aarav's story reminds us that crypto wealth isn't built in a weekend. It's built in *weeks, months, years* — of intention, discipline, and intelligent risk. With a clear goal, a simple structure, and consistent action, anyone can create a 5-year plan that leads to real freedom.

Your story starts the same way his did — with a decision. Make it today. Build your system. Follow it. Adjust along the way. And five years from now, you could be standing at the edge of your own new life — free, focused, and finally in control.

From Digital Dreams to Lasting Freedom

Crypto may have started as an experiment — a radical idea scribbled into a whitepaper by a pseudonymous figure — but today, it's a global force reshaping how we think about money, ownership, and opportunity. It's easy to get caught up in charts, cycles, and technology. But at its core, the crypto economy is about something deeply human: *freedom.* The freedom to own your future. To control your destiny. To exit broken systems and build something better.

This book wasn't written to tell you what token to buy or when to sell. It was written to help you build something far more valuable: a mindset. A strategy. A roadmap. One that lasts longer than any bull run or bear cycle. Because wealth — real wealth — isn't measured in your portfolio's peak. It's measured in the peace you feel knowing that you're no longer playing someone else's game.

If you've made it this far, you're not just a reader. You're a builder. A believer. Someone who sees through the noise and understands the quiet power of compound action. You know now that small, consistent decisions beat big emotional swings. That planning beats panic. And that true wealth requires both courage and control.

Maybe you're just beginning your journey with a few hundred dollars and a whole lot of questions. Or maybe you've already built a solid portfolio and are looking for the next step. Either way, your success will come from *how you think*, *how you adapt*, and *how you execute* — not from predicting the market or chasing hype.

You've seen the stories. The people who started with $1,000 and ended up with six-figure portfolios. The single moms who built financial independence with stablecoins. The DAO contributors who turned passion into purpose. The farmers, teachers, and freelancers from Lagos, Buenos Aires, Manila, and beyond — building in silence, learning as they go, and shaping the next financial era.

Crypto doesn't care where you were born. It doesn't care about your resume. It rewards curiosity. Discipline. Patience. And action. It punishes greed and ego. And it elevates those who build, give, and lead with clarity.

What comes next is entirely up to you. You can walk away from this book inspired but unchanged. Or you can open your calendar, create your dashboard, write your five-year goals, and begin building — slowly, quietly, powerfully.

Because five years from now, the world will be different. New protocols will rise. New empires will be built. Millions more will be onboarded. And wealth will flow to those who didn't wait for permission. Who didn't wait for the news to catch up. Who made their move when things were still uncertain.

You have the tools. You have the blueprint. Now you have the responsibility. The future of wealth isn't waiting. It's being created right now — by people just like you.

So build. Share. Teach. Invest wisely. And when you look back one day at the life you've created, may it be proof that you didn't just ride the wave — you *designed the ocean.*

You're not just part of a financial revolution.

You're part of a *wealth awakening*.

www.ingramcontent.com/pod-product-compliance
Lightning Source LLC
LaVergne TN
LVHW022014200926
848481LV00007B/2386